Praise

*for Cherie Kephart and
Poetry of Peace*

"Visceral, gritty, and laced with rich metaphor, Cherie captures us in these beautiful verses and takes us beyond our usual trance into the very essence of what the earthly sojourn is about—descending into the dark depths which we dread, and tracing back to the Infinity that we discover we really are."

—Suresh Ramaswamy
author of *Just Be* and teacher of *Transform Your Life*

"Cherie Kephart's words sing with an honest, and often raw, clarity. *Poetry of Peace* is a tapestry of love and desire, despair and loneliness, the challenges of surviving life. Approach this collection as you would a gourmet meal: prepare for the extraordinary."

—Clifton King
author of *Poetry Organic*

"*Poetry of Peace* is the olive branch carried by the dove of peace, opening us to the beauty that is all Life. Enlivening the extraordinary in the ordinary, the miracles in the mundane. The heart can rest and rise in these words, for they carry the sacred that is at the core of each moment, reminding us that we are already home."

—Nicole Martel, M.A.
transformational breath and
holistic wellness practitioner

"Cherie's poems transport us to a depth within ourselves that connects us to something vast and sacred. It is as if she has access to a language we have not fully learned yet, and she finds just the right combination of ingredients to satiate and delight. Be prepared to fall in love over and over again as you journey through this rich collection."

—Shelley McQuerter
founder & director of
Learn Homeopathy Now

"From the depths of her soul, Cherie shares with you her unique journey; each poem takes you down a different path of her life, exposing you to her very core, peeling back every emotion, every thought, and placing you in that very moment with her. As she continues to battle, to grow, to transform and to heal, you are able to journey with her and see why she is the gifted writer she is today. This is a different kind of masterpiece—it's *Poetry for Peace*."

—Tenia Bentley
holistic health practitioner

"It is good to have poems such as these, words that slow us up for just a bit, to steady or unsettle us, amidst the language where we live."

—Sandy Carpenter
poet and writing teacher

"This is a beautiful collection of poetry that takes us through the journey of life in all its beauty—dark and light, hard and soft, sad and happy. All of life's journeys are unique to each of us, yet the words on these pages sing true for us all."

—Asa Wild
artist and fellow explorer

"*Poetry of Peace* is, at times, soft and tender, at others, the rawness is accosting. Through all the suffering and the seeking, Cherie's greatest strength is in simultaneous perseverance and surrender. 'Be who you are, not who you were,' she writes, and with hard-earned wisdom realizes, 'the only way out is the way back in.' As fortune favors the brave, Cherie ultimately leaves us uplifted with the words of her physical, mental, emotional, and spiritual liberation."

—Eliza Rhodes
author of *Sign Language*

Poetry of Peace

CHERIE KEPHART

BAZI PUBLISHING

Bazi Publishing
San Diego, CA
BaziPublishing.com

Copyright © Cherie Kephart, 2018
All Rights Reserved.

No part of this book may be reproduced by any mechanical, photographic, or electronic process; nor may it be stored in a retrieval system, transmitted, or otherwise be copied for public or private use—other than for "fair use" as brief quotations embodied in articles and reviews—without prior written permission of the author. Thank you for buying an authorized copy of this book and for complying with copyright laws.

For more information, email bazi@bazipublishing.com or visit BaziPublishing.com

PUBLISHER'S CATALOGING-IN-PUBLICATION DATA

Names: Kephart, Cherie, author.

Title: Poetry of peace / Cherie Kephart.

Description: San Diego, CA : Bazi Publishing, [2018]

Identifiers: ISBN: 978-1-947127-09-8 (paperback) |
978-1-947127-10-4 (ePub) | 978-1-947127-11-1 (Mobi) |
LCCN: 2018906329

Subjects: LCSH: Poetry, American. | Poetry--Women authors. | Love poetry--Women authors. | Peace--Poetry. | Healing--Poetry. | Well-being--Poetry. | Health--Poetry. | Spirituality--Poetry. | Inspiration--Poetry. | Mind and body--Poetry. | Spirit--Poetry. | Change (Psychology)--Poetry. | Self-realization--Poetry. | Self-actualization (Psychology)--Poetry. | LCGFT: Poetry. | Love poetry. | BISAC: POETRY / American / General. | POETRY / Women Authors. | POETRY / Subjects & Themes / Death, Grief, Loss. | POETRY / Subjects & Themes / Inspirational & Religious. | POETRY / Subjects & Themes / Nature. | POETRY / Subjects & Themes / Love & Erotica.

Classification: LCC: PS3611.E694 P64 2018 | DDC: 811/.6--dc23

Other titles: Kephart, Cherie. Few minor adjustments. The Healing 100.

Printed in the United States of America
10 9 8 7 6 5 4 3 2 1

Cover Art: Cherie Kephart
Book Jacket & Interior Page Design: Asa Wild at asawild.org

for the beauty of peace

ABOUT
Poetry of Peace

My life has been about ascension. I have traveled from the innocence of a child filled with wonder, aspirations, and belief in the impossible, to the deepest depths of darkness.

Harnessing the strength of spirit, I found my way through the shadows. I came to understand that no matter how bleak life becomes, there is always light, and peace remains within. At times, it has been forgotten, or difficult to retrieve, but it never leaves. Now I reopen my eyes and heart and become a child once again.

May you be open to the world and truly see it, be brave and steady as you encounter darkness, breathe deep as you move into light, and embrace grace as you arrive once again with peace.

"The wound is the place where the Light enters you."
—Rumi

CONTENTS

1	*Seeing the World*	
	3	Wonder
	4	Child in My Life
	5	Feats
	6	Dreams
	8	I Wish…
	9	Colorful
	10	Complicated
	12	If You Were Here
	14	One More Time
	15	Stay
	16	I See…
	17	I Am…
	18	Listen
	20	Change
	22	Rhetoric of a Tree
	24	Warm Me
	25	Night Flower

27 *Through Darkness*

- 29 Pretending
- 30 Walking Wounded
- 32 A lone
- 33 Without
- 34 Sinful
- 36 Why?
- 38 Goodbye
- 39 Mercy
- 40 Lunatic
- 42 Lemonade
- 43 Behind
- 44 Edge
- 46 Black Eyes, Black Heart
- 48 Running in Place
- 50 Winter
- 52 Maybe
- 54 Drift
- 56 Tumbling
- 57 Air
- 58 Not My Own
- 59 A Little While
- 60 A Past
- 61 To Live Again

63 *Into the Light*
- 65 The Ride
- 66 Unknown
- 67 Ascension
- 68 Be What?
- 69 Being
- 70 Legacy of Us
- 71 Lost in the Miracle
- 72 Haiku 1
- 72 Haiku 2
- 73 Haiku 3
- 73 Haiku 4
- 74 No Today
- 75 Me Alone
- 76 The Way I Do
- 77 Way Out
- 78 Together
- 79 Alive
- 80 Everywhere
- 82 Daybreak

85 *With Peace*
- 87 Decision
- 88 Gentle Rain
- 89 Awakened
- 90 Abounding Garden
- 91 Hawaiian Sky
- 92 Heat
- 93 More
- 94 Lifted
- 96 New Beginning
- 98 One Day
- 99 Soar
- 100 You…
- 101 None
- 102 After All

105 GRATITUDE
109 ABOUT THE AUTHOR
113 ALSO BY CHERIE KEPHART
115 STAY INVOLVED

Seeing the World

Wonder

I wonder if the moon makes sense
on the other side of the stars
or the night's solemn blackness
tells tales of more than slumber.

I wonder how dolphins sing shrill
tones vibrating into the world
no two moments of sound the same
a composition I cannot follow.

But I understand the sun.
Its rhythmic warmth and healing
gifted to all, radiating love
beyond all measure.

I hope to wake up one day and be
the sun so I can feel what it's like
to live with grace.

Child in My Life

I am a child in the theater of my life
the beginner, hoping, waiting for exposure
to the wholesome wonders of the world.

I reset my mind to blankness
and know I am young again.

I believe in all I see and hear
it is wise to be naïve.

To realize radiance for the first
time for anything, always.

The mind knows no past and feels
at ease, open, and released into light.

I am the child in the theater of my life
my actions simple, honest, and loving
let me be free, I roar, and let me be me.

Feats

I feel the richness of the grass like silk
beneath my feet. *You are welcome
here*, the green blades say. And so I walk
over the feats of fallen lyricists entombed
in this field, their forever home.

Dirt and stone shield their eyes, they are blind
to the wild weeds that shroud their bodies,
swaddle their creative minds; these minds
so raptly regarded time over inspired time.

All these legends, where I now stand
on their land, yield to my breath
where my words will tread
where my feats will be known.

DREAMS

Dreams gained
are those dreamt awake.

Notice how the lake
holds the reflection
of the mysterious
white mountains.

These little moments
hold great triumph
whisper their legacy
into my soul.

Observe the heron
basking in the stillness
of the early morning
before the day begins.

Perceive of the harmony
in each broad breath
healthy heartbeat
and sonorous sigh.

Dreams lost become
sunshine of another day.

I Wish...

you could see what my eyes see
your tender transcendent soul hypnotizing
mine. I hear the noise of my own voice
in yours. Roaring, it wrestles with your heart.

I wish...

we could be together in silence under
that majestic star-strewn sky, dwarfing
both you and me.

I wish...

we could move together in ways only
our two souls know how and bathe
in the oneness of us, our beauty
never to fade.

Colorful

I am
more than
cream bones in a shell
grey inside my skull
blue of my veins
white of my cells.

I am
green pastures of hope
recycled yellow streaks
of cowardice for some
purple majesty fortified
with red badges of courage.

COMPLICATED

My heart is...
complicated.

My heart is...
infused with lust
burdened with grief
laced with passion
obscured by despair
fueled by desire
strangled by fear
lifted by love
arrested by anger.

My heart...
beats fiercely
breaks slowly
gains momentum
loses its rhythm
falls short of a miracle
leaves me no choice
obeys my soul
betrays my mind.

My heart is...
complicated.

If You Were Here

Leaves drift
like nothing before
and never again
against your skin.

Pale blotches
around your eyes
I would remember
if you were here.

I die every day
just to wake up
next to you.

I remain youthful
but adventure
escapes my bones.

I'm aged
but not ready
for permanent sleep.

Goodbye drips
from your mouth…
I would remember
if you were here.

One More Time

Simply move on
and again wonder,
how did I get here?
One day it will be over
and it will be fine,
like the night lifted
by dawn given to rise
again in someone else's sky.

Stay

Inside the walls of a vacant room, her long
bony fingers stretch out across the keys.
Her heavy breath collides with the jarring
discord she creates. The music is no more.

*Show me how the rain cascades down
the mountains of your sacred soul*, she
softly sighs. *Show me the years gone astray
the ones of yesterday, for there is hardly
a ghost left for me to talk with anymore.*

*Please, pull up that old chair, press
the glass to your lips, drink the coolness
into your voice, then sing for me! Frolic
in your senses, neglect your place in this
space, and stay here with me in antiquity.*

I See...

the depth
without the tools
to know.

Wisdom rests
on forgetting
our thoughts
and realizing
the quiet truths.

I see the depth
without the tools
to know...

and I see everything.

I Am...

a shadow. Afraid of the light.
Oppressed by sudden movements.

I am a storm. A surge of eruptions.
Strength laced with erratic emotions.

I am a galaxy. Fogginess floating.
Absent in space and time.

I am a thought. Born of delusion.
Words and gestures taken to heart.

In the I's of the world, I am nothing.
But in my eyes, I am everything.

LISTEN

You'll hear the chair
utter
sit upon my fabric
relax your thoughts
leave them with me.

You'll hear the table
shout
use my timber
for your expensive taste
savor the moment on me.

You'll hear the book
articulate
absorb my words
expand your reality
become someone new.

You'll hear the pen
proclaim
employ my ink
craft your ideas
unleash your urges.

Oh, scribe of emotions
we're all here for you
they exclaim
if you just listen.

Change

I imagine the infinite light
but I can't see it
I drown in the dimness
it is definite and dim.

Chrome crowds my mind
the shiny stuff that
doesn't matter
but you think it does.

I don't have logic anymore.

I left it on the stairs
behind the shed
out back near the creek
anywhere but with me.

Grass grows beneath
my toes, tangled and torn
razor-sharp and I realize
I haven't moved this season.

He takes my hand. Change.

And the ground shifts
under me and the whales
know my song
even if he doesn't.

I'll leave you to the morning
tea and muesli dripping with flavors
of walnut and cinnamon,
more again I am like you.

Rhetoric of a Tree

Dew descends in designs
sending out messages
from my branches.
Can you hear me?

Sharp inflated speech
the fallen leaves
of my thoughts.
Do I make a sound?

Absence of a tongue
detracts not from conviction
I still taste the moisture.
What do I say?

Fresh plum blossoms hang
the fragrant birth of illusion.
Temporal and finite.
Could I mean this?

I too will be cut
haggard and worn
saws and dust as the rest.
What next from me?

An obtuse obituary.

Warm Me

That old green ceramic
mug you gave me
is empty, give or take
a drop or two. More
tea to warm it please
for life is so cold.

Night Flower

The onyx beauty rises and sinks
in the throat of the shadowy marsh
quieted by the virtue of sovereign muses
anchored in the doldrums of captivity.

Its petals gasp and wail in silence
mirrored only by the broad dark space
lingering between the sullen stars.
It pleads for freedom, a license to soar.

Break through creature, break through!
But your life is not for liberty
your existence is merely an exhibit
a facade of harmony and grace.

Your spirit encased in exquisite detail
yet haunted by the fortitude of stillness.
Your plight so painfully palpable
even the slain creatures at your roots
grieve for your imprisonment,
for at least they once had wings to fly.

Through Darkness

Pretending

In the windowless night I search
for the stars as I do every time
I come to this moment. But something
is broken inside me, thrashed like
the shattered shore after a storm.

I disappear into a sea of people
my shoulders hunched, hiding
my dreams inside my head.
Pretending. I fly so high hoping
I won't ever land. But I do.

I always do.

Walking Wounded

My eyes, covered with blindness
yet I see the velvety green leaves
on the tree. My ears, drenched
in deafness, yet I hear the birds
chirping sweetly toward the sky.

My heart, impregnated by darkness
yet I feel love. My legs, shrouded
in pain, yet I walk, wounded among
the living. Alive, I am, but I am also
dead. I am the walking wounded.

I am the crawling patient, ailing
friend, desperate daughter, lonely
drifter among my departed dreams.
I am the walking wounded.

I am the giftless neighbor, fallen
writer, barren lover, outraged
woman in my wretched space.
I am the walking wounded.

Dead, I am, but I am also alive.

A LONE

gaze
see me
listen
hear me
think
know me
run
leave me
stranded
alone

you
call it
wisdom

unloved

I call it
pain

Without

my pen leaks passion
for memories I no
longer know

fondness slips away
everything is a facade
with my eyes closed
I watch the distance
arrive before my sight

when I know the ink
intimately I feel more
than I could say without
words

it leaks
it drips
it gives
but not to me

Sinful

Let us begin! Select a sin
with or without intent.
Either weighs the same
always one hundred percent.

Scorched by lust
you feed on fire
a loathsome hunger
a lurid desire.

Encumbered by envy
you exude evil
a burden so heavy
a constant upheaval.

Gluttony and greed
are gruesome and ghastly
gorgeous in the moment
but ultimately nasty.

Persecuted by pride
you percolate persuasion
a pompous and putrid
outward invasion.

Wrath and sloth
are weighty and soiled
a scandalous display
of a soul spoiled.

Do you sense the stench
the scent of sin
the sickening smell
of consequence?

If not yet, you will.

Why?

Garments hang loose on my bones
my face vivid hues of pink
I've walked these floors before
tranquil moments before
the sun gets a chance to rise
and the shadows full of secrets
slide across your freckled face.

You lie, tucked beneath blankets
barely breathing through the
darkness. My heart pounds
like a hostile hammer, ill-equipped
to continue the beats ahead.

The air dances between us
without beauty or grace
I'm a child without a jacket
my mother insisted I take
a dolphin deprived of waters
in which to swim. I am lost
in the wreckage of what I no
longer feel, no longer believe,
no longer know.

You, barely breathing between
the blankets of darkness
while my, my heart yearns
and whispers with worship.

Goodbye

Mangled in the shards
of sanity, I fly as a blue bird
or a bee, yes, yes, a bee! I fly
fast from stem to bud
of a bloom. I suck the pollen
from you while the perch awaits
my song and waits for my words
that speak of silence, yet your
mouth always says what I am
never ready to hear.

Mercy

he wears black
blue trim on his
converse high-tops
the letters across
his chest read
Mercy…
Mercy…
Mercy…
Mercy for animals
oh yes
I pound my chest
mercy for the animal
in me

LUNATIC

And he shouts with conviction,
*Everyone below me know not
what it is to be me.* His nostrils
flare, his voice deepens,
As if they could, he sneers.

Through his snake-like eyes
and a backwards smile
his hatred heightens as
toxic thoughts enrage him.

What deluded souls wish
to ensnare my evil existence?
Are you not also my victims?
Moral or sinister, sick or sane,
is it not all the same?

Can it be understood
the madness of his matter?
For such behavior they
release their hounds
obedient souls loyal
to a cause set before them.

Others stand beside him
with equally deceptive minds
but there is no care among them.
His actions create a rare taste
savored only by himself.

Alone, the lunatic boils.
He skulks beyond their grasp
even if he is caught.
His life is not in this world.
His is in another.

Lemonade

I cannot taste the lemonade
derived from the sour fruit,
the bitterness eludes
my failing senses. An air
of acid showers me, only
the rotten seeds of demise
remain.

Behind

Pleasure isn't home anymore;
vacant and uninspired. Sorrow
of the daily breath continues,
out   then   in.

Repeat.

Even when joy has faded
hidden in the shadows of
mirth and pretense.
Out   then   in.

Repeat.

But I can leave it all behind.
It is now, and has always been
my choice.
Out   then…

EDGE

Have you ever thought
about what happened
to me after that night?

I crawled out
of the cesspool
you call passion
stood on the edge
one moment
fading into another

black

and the thump
thump   here...
lost all its power

I can't hear it
anymore
ever since you
moved inside me
you didn't ask
you took

I screamed
you liked it more
left me dripping

black

not enough rain
to wash away
this shame
not enough blood
to rid the damage

I live in the gutter
of your lust
I stand on the edge
thinking
this can't be
what life is for.

Black Eyes, Black Heart

Wrath. Prevalent.
Thriving in my blood.
Demons. Fierce.
Racing in my mind.
There is no light.

Wisdom. Contaminated.
Exiting my soul.
Thoughts. Defiled.
Departing my brain.
There is no light.

Dungeons of grey. Pillars of iron.
Wrap around me.
Beasts of prey. Parasites of flesh.
Seek to kill me.
There is no light.

My eyes quiver.
Blackness approaches.
My heart rages.
Blackness persists.
My spirit dies.
Blackness takes over.
There is no light.

Running in Place

My heart slows me down, interrupts my stride
I unsheathe my sword and strike.
The severed veins next to my heart
leak passion and bow shyly as wet swans.
Weight of my blood engulfs my desires,
pressing my soul deep into the earth.

I watch my arms, rapidly moving.
But in my truthful gloom
they fall motionless to the floor.
I hope for my legs,
yet they are infused with decay.
Deplorable creatures feast on my flesh.

My final faith lies with the wind
to pick me up and carry me away.
But the air is still,
a haunting silence surrounding my breath.
And so the blood continues to pour
draining my life force,
extracting the entrails of my once beloved shell.

The assault of purple liquid flowing into red
bombards my sapphire eyes.
I shiver with the knowledge
of what is next to come.
The rise of my last seconds
the descent of my voyage into silence.

My thoughts circle
devouring my demise.
And I then realize
as I drift out of this life
I am running in place,
just as I have always been.

Winter

Your face is like winter
cold and barren
icicles hang
from your throat
giving me no sense
of your truth.

My face is like autumn
golden and warm
feelings fall
from my core
unable to keep
them safe inside.

I release them
unceremoniously
toward your snow
filled heart
I'm crushed.

Maybe one day
you'll turn into spring
I'll lapse into summer
and we'll meet there.

Maybe

Maybe…
I'll sail a ship into some somber
scant station of my soul
resurrect the radiance of rage
and flaunt the innocence of my guilt.

Maybe…
I'll ignore the yellow discharge
surging from my spine
and paint the town a fancy
shade of red, riding with my hood
somewhere over that rainbow.

Maybe…
I'll release the weak stronghold
on the warped fortress I call mine
watch where I step, for it may blow
my perceptions into petty pieces.

Maybe…
I'll truly live from within, not from
without[side] my box of dark chocolate
sugar-filled treats that I never seem
to get enough or let go of.

And maybe, while I'm there
I'll even learn to truly love myself.

Then again…

DRIFT

sometimes wounds
don't ever heal
no matter how many
wishes on a star
candles on a cake
or pleading prayers
on bleeding knees…
time simply doesn't
tick   tick   tick
them away

sometimes we stand still
while we crash
sometimes we drift until
we are defeated
then taught to rise again

maybe our dreams
are moving too fast
maybe we
should be moving too

we stand with our mistakes
in our hands
our fists clenched
oozing self-pity

and the taste of heat
on our tongues
sizzles and slithers
like a serendipitous snake
sensing our screams

subtract the silence from ourselves
exorcise the hell from our eyes
avert our gaze
from the maze of malice that wraps us
and devours our intentions.

Drift no more.

TUMBLING

Sinking and descending
to the edge of my life,
I sit on the empty ground
of my history.
I am left, waiting.
Waiting, for another chance.

Rising and floating to
my last breath,
the reckless winds of life
twirl and shake my future.
I am left, wondering.
Wondering, what if.

Shifting and staggering
along the road of ruins,
I suffer from the grimness
of a silent forever.
I am left, tumbling.
Tumbling, with no end.

AIR

In the thick, scalding sweetness of the air
I reach for my breath. It slithers. Vanishes.

The sharp squeak of the back door we never
fixed reminds me you aren't coming home.
Deflated like a child's mishandled balloon
my helpless heart matches that pitchy squeal
and faintly wheezes a wretched sigh.

In the thin, scalding bitterness of the air
you no longer care.

Not My Own

I scream the song of silence
and release the brutish beast
that is my bursting breath
this still water that I thirst
for in the dread of my life.

I ask the white doves of clarity
help me see not with my eyes
but with the deep pulse of my heart.
Lift my intent to romance my own soul
into refined blossoms of beauty.

Once bemused and apocalyptic
my mind now knows the nature
of my struggle. These doubts
these fears that I have carried
through dark decades of somber strife
are not even my own.

A Little While

I fumble through fantasies of past lifetimes
and come up slow like a desert blossom.
Saturated by the beaming golden dawn
brilliant and sentient light unveils
what happens between my head and heart.

I remove the Tarbuck knot from the end
of my noose and the pity-drenched gag
from inside my mouth. I release my senses
to the sense of the world, my mind screams
in tangerine and green; these colors make me smile.

I do believe I've changed my mind. Think I'll
stay on this earth for yet still a little while.

A Past

I used to
ties me to my past.

A past I cannot escape from.
Ever.

A past I cannot run from.
Ever.

A past I can only learn from.
Always.

Time to move past
my past.

To Live Again

I sit alone wrapped tight in my insecurity
a heated blanket soft upon my shrinking skin.
It keeps me far from the places I long to go.

I recognize this place in my mind, I know it.
The cowardice that drags me back inside
my sheer shell, sweeps away all my courage.

Once intoxicated, sprightly as a child, my heart
now languishes, an inert glacier afraid to melt
burned by life's bitter consequences.

I do recognize this place. I do know it.
I still loathe it. So, I twist this fate
into a flowering new spring, pick up my foolish
self and struggle to bloom once again.

Into the Light

The Ride

The ambulance ride is as exquisite
as a day at the beach, for in the ambulance
I am alert, acutely aware that I am still alive,
that these moments embody essence.

And I am paying attention.

Almost losing you, this body, is like awakening
to the magnitude of inhalation. Each second,
every pulse, each glance from another soul
announces, the moment is now.

And I am paying attention.

Unknown

Rosettes, the color of peaches
decorate my wearied senses
fragrant reminders of it all.
Lost now, beyond my grasp
like a maze of cold concrete
desolate and worn; unknown.

Ascension

Sometimes I forget to whisper
those dusty words intended
to float from my lips.

I shout the song of the sparrow
without the verses
for the sound weighs most.

The pulse of being ignites
the powerful essence eager
to edge out into the earth.

Sometimes I remember to release
the blockage of doubt
meant to hold me in place.

And so, I soar sweetly sideways
unto the swell of the living
secrecy softly shattered.

I open my breath and ascend.

BE WHAT?

This lonely afternoon of mangled memories
offers no solace for my polluted brain.
Irksome images flaunt themselves
licking clean the inside of my thoughts
like the tenacious tongue of a famished fly.

Two types of memories waltz swiftly
crosswise the corners of my mind
those that are true and those fabricated
to conceal what I dare not remember.
I can no longer separate them. They collide
like the teeth of a shark upon helpless prey.

A voice inside me shouts, *Why hold on*
to what you've done? It destroys you.
Even your molded mementos cannot save you.
Renounce the relentless perceptions of yourself.
Be power, be change, be—, then silence.
Be what? I ask with haste. *Be what?*

With a solemn, deep breath, the voice whispers,
Be who you are, not who you were.

Being

a breeze
in my coffin
delight of day
brings me closer
to being
another way

Legacy of Us

your touch follows
my impervious senses
to an unpaved
road of passion
sweet and slow
I fall into your arms
a flower of the dawn
shadows of the night
giving thanks for our light
of wisdom it shines
without grace   gifts
starved of all of it
never for us
or around us
simply onto us
and then away
dark forever
floating beyond
our eyes into never
known lands of space

LOST IN THE MIRACLE

The fuse of my spirit
burns bright as the dawn
after a battle of blood
soldiers of pain   eager
emotions from wayward
minds in the forest of life
trees blind my sight
and leaves fall against
my feet   the rough
feel of decay crackling
against my bare skin
lost in the miracle of time
I find what is inside.

Haiku

Haiku 1

I'm not a bargain
I am full strength one hundred
fifty percent proof

Haiku 2

the chains clank and clink
'round your creative chatter
creep coward retreat

Haiku 3

cancel the chaos
console the sole of your soul
rejoice in your voice

Haiku 4

I kiss the shadows
and vault into adventure
squeezing the sunshine

No Today

I carry you in my senses
your smile in my frown
your voice in my ears
your lips in my eyes

seduced by your grace
I escape the dungeons
of my thoughts and leap
into tomorrow as if today
did not exist.

Me Alone

Alone feels right
the splendor of my own
smile, shine of my eyes
as I witness the truth
my truth.

My solo trek in the yard
of forgotten yearnings
mirrors in clear view
a land of languished love
a sky of secret serenades
years of giving beyond
what I could—never receiving
generosity toward the self
of me, the center of light
needed to glow and grow.

Now I perceive
it is me I need
to adore and it
will always be
me alone.

The Way I Do

Your smile sends sunshine
to me with piercing grace
like the yellow of bananas
swinging from the wisdom
of brown brawny branches
that know how to hold on
and precisely when to let go
the way I never do.

As your light sweeps across
my thoughts, I wade through
a pool of blue and travel
to such places, mishandle them
the letting go, the moving on
rootless and impressionable
the way I always do.

Way Out

with fields of frost
beneath my feet
I step out onto the
boulevard of bones
cracked and hollow
stale and dry

for a moment
my desire rises
and then it is gone
an ambush of thoughts
startle me as I realize
the only way out
is the way back in

TOGETHER

I swear the sun shines brighter over us.
Drowning in desire, craggy cliffs of peril
wrap around my chest. What an exquisite
way to die. Lacerated by lust and love,
I doubt the garden's green grass has ever
been so sharp, ever stood so tall
as when you and I walk in it

together.

ALIVE

I break the glass
climb through a tree
into the seductive sky
shatter, shatter me.

A canyon of hope
awaits the other side
adorned with salvation
alive, alive.

Everywhere

I saunter down an ocean trail
my retinas burn from the sights around me.
A crushed snail slaughtered by a footprint.
An earthworm hardened from the heat.
A squashed squirrel sprawled on the street.
A grief-stricken woman seeks solace
from the speechless shrill of the sunshine.
Up toward the sky I look for reprieve
a hawk circles, searches for its next prey.

Death is everywhere.

I trudge through the coarse sand.
Glance at my watch. One hour of peace.
Cross-legged on the sturdy earth
I thrust the tan granules through my toes
and arch my back toward the sun.
My ears celebrate the roar of the tide
sweeping in and out before me.

Life, you are not beautiful, exactly.

The hour closes. I amble to my car.
This time my eyes notice more.
Aromatic blossoms boisterous and bright.
Toddlers wobble, guileless and wild.
Teenage lovers lock in a lustful kiss.
Sparrows squawk, swooping
childishly in the cloudless air.
In a mirthful moment of epiphany
the murkiness of the world fades.

Life is everywhere.

Daybreak

I enter bitter daybreak
an encounter of scorn
as the allure of white
perfumed lilacs sing
in replete resignation
shower me, shower me.
Ah! The sweetness
of the sun shines
brightly upon me.
Alone, no more.

Decision

...is twisted in the road
from my heart and head.

And I walk small through
the forest of dark thoughts
asking to be shown the path

yet it is only when I stand
tall that I make my own

way to the place
illuminated by peace.

GENTLE RAIN

Bright as glass, inexhaustible and true
is everything in me and everything in you.
Genuine as the gentle rain that descends
in decorative designs upon gardens of green
our souls reveal a precipitous peace.
A sanctuary of luminosity, the flawless
love exchanged moves me from this earthly
plane: we are alive with spirit, we are one.

Awakened

Beneath a blackened sky
I see the sunrise in your eyes
a sublime expanse of serenity
serenading the siren song in me.

I have seen your benevolent eyes
before, a prism through which I have
tasted truth, a familiar feeling
like solace under a sacred tree.

Awakened by the alchemy of us
I embrace tranquility, a moment divine
the light of spirit encased in the power
of our gaze, a bliss-filled bounty of peace
for now and in all ways.

Abounding Garden

Outside, wise burly fruit trees in mist and rain
celebrate their dampened leaves.

Outside, sweet butterflies in the sunshine
sing praise for their expansive wings.

Outside, insects in long blades of green
march headstrong into the autumn breeze.

Inside, a soul wrapped in tranquil meditation
chants a symphony of celestial tones
Namaste, Namaste, Namaste.

Hawaiian Sky

An apotheosis of captivity.
A lurch, a bottle of forgiveness
a vase filled with visual grace.
These gifts of anything but gold
the essence of rawness and truth
speak to me in courageous strides.

Incandescence of the stars.
Jupiter, he shines brightly.
My bare eyes cannot see him
yet I bask in his untouchable warmth
projected from his prominent glow.
He lifts the lightness within me.

Tranquility of the rain.
Drops on Kona fields, nestled
in palm leaves, a spectrum
of brightness left behind.
All that was me is forgotten
my renewed soul forges ahead.

HEAT

In the fresh depths of dawn
I listen to the crisp wonder
of the sun and swim in the
flood of its heat. My eyes
salute its boundless grace
the impression that once it could
be touched. This hour is now.
Now for you, now for me,
now for the sister moon.
The ardent air both heals and
scorches, but nothing comes
close to the essence of your
sacred soul. Each day anew as
the one before, appetent of divine
thirst, eternally, our deepest
passions are quenched.

MORE

Streams of golden heat
wrap around my skin.
Rain. Rain. Rain.
No, sun! Shine upon me.

A pillow of guileless grace
flows into the portal of my
mind as I realize in each goodbye
there is hello.

Farewell daffodils and damp drops
of peace who find me, lure me.
I quiet myself deep within so I
can hear more of what is not said.

LIFTED

My feet shuffle
across the sand
my lungs fill
with the crisp air
of the coast
my senses reel.

Fused
with delicate
balance
of the ocean
waves   my being
is lifted.

This night
transcends
all boundaries
leaving me
awake
to my future.

I am floating
through courageous
melodies
nature's peace
powerful moments
lifting me to now.

New Beginning

Two souls meet, adjacent a tangerine sun
beneath a tranquil Hawaiian heaven.
A serendipitous encounter, I murmur.
No coincidences on earth, the shaman affirms.
Comfortable, she asks. I nod, relaxed.

Her healing tools, poised around us.
A primal drum with an enchanting hum
protective snake with gilded eyes
mystical flute bears the tune of angels
ancient stones luminous as the skies.

Sweet passenger, she declares,
hold true. Forceful waves will heave
your soul in a staunch unrest. It is there,
on the ledge of life, as you let go of the last
branch, that your path will finally begin.

My body encircled by serene sensations
aromatic arches of energy surround me
powerful parables parade around my being.
Unnerved, I fidget, the intensity accelerates.
I am transcended. I am transformed. I am now.

One Day

I move through the moonstruck mist
deep in the crest of the cloud forest
yet my legs are as still as the stars.

One day I will be released.

I pursue the parade of pink petals
countless flowers in the fields of grace
yet my eyes are shielded from sight.

One day I will see.

I throw off every word I ever wore
each declaration I ever swore.
Each thought I've held on to, I've left
them all behind, freed my mind.

One day is today.

Soar

And you soar with the flight
of those that have passed
and you dream
of the visions to come
and your strength
is granted from the farms
of the sky
and the riches of the trees
forever reaching high
and you soar

forever more.

You...

rattle the sunshine
caress the moon
sway slow soft with sounds
as you parade and push
your hips through clothes
out into the world
with a peaceful proclamation
here I am

once again.

None

There are no corners in my mind
    no boundaries in my heart.
No edges to my body
    no limits to my soul.

There are no peaks to my imagination
    no ceilings to my thoughts.
No heights to my love
    no confines to my life.

There are none.

After All

Sometimes my blood
whispers regret
for all I have known.
All that I have seen.

But I know
in each moment
there is everything.

Darkness and light.
Pain and bliss.
Fear and assurance.
Loneliness and love.

And I realize
sometimes it is just
my turn to suffer.

And of course
sometimes it is
my turn to shine.

I include the shadows
as I ride the next wave
plunge into the future
and after all, affirm

it is again my turn to live!

Gratitude

Like the hills of my heart,
some have crumbled,
others swept away.
Through all the destruction,
amidst the confusion,
engulfed in the trenches
of lasting pain, I am blessed.

I am blessed because of you,
the strangers whose smiles
catch my eyes and absorb
these words. The animals
whose pure love reaches my
soul. The trees, daisies, rain,
and stars that confirm delight.

I am blessed because of you,
my friends, my family,
who hold me up to reach
my highest and best self.
For all the comfort, laughter,
support, and kindness, I am
alive and with peace because of you.

With gratitude evermore,
Cherie

About the Author

Cherie Kephart is a writer, artist, and poet. Raised in Venice, California, Cherie longed to travel and experience the way other people lived. After serving as a Peace Corps volunteer in Zambia on a water sanitation and health education project, Cherie returned to the United States with an African souvenir she didn't expect: a mysterious illness. She fell severely ill and almost died, leaving her with several symptoms that went undiagnosed for many years. This inspired Cherie to write her memoir, *A Few Minor Adjustments: A Memoir of Healing*, taking the reader on a powerful but entertaining journey through her adventures and search for life-saving answers.

Her memoir has won several awards and received an outpouring of heartfelt responses, motivating Cherie to write a companion book, *The Healing 100: A Practical Guide to Transforming Your Body, Mind, and Spirit*.

Since first absorbing the magnificent words of John Keats when she was a child, Cherie yearned to write poetry—to share her thoughts and her own rhythm of language with the world. To realize her dream as a poet spawns music in her soul. *Poetry of Peace* chronicles her discovery of healing at both a deeper and a higher level.

Cherie has earned a Masters in Medical and Cultural Anthropology and has been celebrated for her holistic approach to healing and her willingness to examine her life lessons in her writing.

Stay connected at: CherieKephart.com

Also By

CHERIE KEPHART

A Few Minor Adjustments: A Memoir of Healing

The Healing 100:
A Practical Guide to Transforming Your Body, Mind, and Spirit

Stay Involved

Connect with Cherie on her Website

CherieKephart.com

Write a Review

for *Poetry of Peace*
CherieKephart.com/review

Connect with Cherie on Social Media

@Cherie.Kephart.Author

Cherie Kephart

@CherieKephart

@CherieKephartWriter

www.ingramcontent.com/pod-product-compliance
Lightning Source LLC
Chambersburg PA
CBHW020140130526
44591CB00030B/168